CW00447392

NEW ROMANIA
TRAVEL GUIDE
2023-2024

*Unveilling the Hidden Gems, Rich Culture,
And Natural Wonders of Romania*

IVAN M. BARBOUR

Copyright

TABLE OF CONTENTS

INTRODUCTION

Welcome to the enchanting land of Romania, where ancient history meets vibrant modernity, and natural wonders unfold at every turn. In this updated travel guide for 2023-2024, we invite you to embark on a captivating journey through this diverse and dynamic country.

Discover the rich tapestry of Romanian culture, from the imposing castles of Transylvania to the lively festivals that echo through the Carpathian Mountains. Experience the warmth of Romanian hospitality in quaint villages and bustling cities alike, and indulge your senses in the country's delectable cuisine, a fusion of traditional flavors and innovative culinary delights.

As you navigate the pages of this guide, you'll find detailed insights into Romania's historical landmarks, picturesque landscapes, and thriving urban centers. Whether you're an adventure seeker, a history buff, a nature enthusiast, or a culinary explorer, Romania has something extraordinary to offer.

In addition to uncovering Romania's tourist gems, this guide provides practical information on planning your trip, navigating the local customs, and ensuring a seamless travel experience. Immerse yourself in the heart of Romania, where legends come to life and every moment is an opportunity for discovery.

So, pack your bags and prepare to be mesmerized. Romania awaits your exploration, promising unforgettable memories and a deep appreciation for the magic that defines this remarkable country.

WHAT'S NEW IN 2023-2024

In the ever-evolving landscape of Romanian tourism, 2023-2024 promises exciting developments and fresh experiences for travelers. Here's a glimpse of what's new and noteworthy:

1. Eco-Friendly Initiatives: Romania continues to emphasize sustainable tourism, with new eco-friendly accommodations, wildlife conservation projects, and efforts to preserve the country's natural beauty.

2. Culinary Innovations: Renowned chefs and local artisans are collaborating to create innovative dishes, blending traditional Romanian flavors with international culinary trends. Explore the burgeoning food scene in both urban hubs and remote villages.

3. Tech-Driven Tourism: Expect enhanced digital guides, augmented reality tours, and immersive smartphone apps that provide interactive experiences, enriching your exploration of historical sites and cultural landmarks.

4. Festivals and Events: Romania's calendar is brimming with exciting festivals celebrating music, arts, and local traditions. Look out for new festivals and events showcasing the country's diverse cultural heritage.

5. Off-The-Beaten-Path Destinations: Discover hidden gems and lesser-known regions as tourism spreads to areas beyond the popular hotspots. Experience the authenticity of rural life and untouched natural beauty in these emerging destinations.

6. Adventure Tourism: Thrill-seekers can rejoice with the introduction of new adventure sports and outdoor activities. From rock climbing in the Carpathians to kayaking adventures in the Danube Delta, there are exhilarating experiences for every adrenaline enthusiast.

7. Heritage Preservation: Restoration efforts are underway in historical sites and heritage buildings, ensuring that visitors can immerse themselves in Romania's rich history while supporting the preservation of cultural landmarks.

8. Connectivity and Accessibility: Improved transportation networks, including new flight routes and upgraded rail services, make it easier than ever to traverse the country, allowing travelers to explore diverse regions with convenience.

Embrace the spirit of adventure and be among the first to uncover these exciting developments in Romania's travel scene in 2023-2024. Your journey promises not only the allure of the familiar but also the thrill of the undiscovered.

TRAVEL TIPS AND ETIQUETTE

Traveling to Romania offers a unique experience, filled with cultural richness and warm hospitality. To make the most of your journey, consider these travel tips and etiquette guidelines:

1. Respect Local Customs: Romanians are proud of their traditions and customs. Respect local practices, especially in rural areas, and be polite when declining offers of food or drinks.

2. Greetings: A firm handshake and maintaining eye contact are common greetings.

Address people with their titles and last names until you are invited to use their first name.

3. Dress Modestly: While urban areas are cosmopolitan, it's respectful to dress modestly, especially when visiting religious sites or rural communities.

4. Language: While many Romanians speak English, learning a few basic Romanian phrases can go a long way in earning respect and making connections with locals.

5. Tipping: Tipping is appreciated but not mandatory. In restaurants, leaving a 10% tip is customary if service is not included. Round up taxi fares and tip hotel staff for exceptional service.

6. Currency: The official currency is the Romanian leu (RON). Inform yourself about the current exchange rates and have some local currency on hand, especially in rural areas.

7. Safety: Romania is generally a safe country, but like anywhere else, be cautious with your belongings, avoid poorly lit areas at night, and be aware of your surroundings.

8. Public Transport: Public transportation is widely available and reliable. Familiarize yourself with local bus and train schedules, and consider using them to explore cities and regions.

9. Cuisine: Romanian cuisine is diverse and delicious. Don't miss the opportunity to try traditional dishes like sarmale (cabbage rolls), mici (grilled sausages), and mămăligă (cornmeal porridge).

10. Photography: Always ask for permission before taking photos of people, especially in rural areas. Some individuals might be sensitive to being photographed.

11. Cultural Sensitivity: Be aware of the country's history, including its communist past.

Avoid sensitive topics in conversations unless the other party initiates such discussions.

By embracing these travel tips and observing local etiquette, you'll not only have a more enjoyable experience but also foster positive interactions with the people you meet along the way. Romania's charm lies not just in its landscapes but also in the warmth of its inhabitants.

CHAPTER 1: GETTING STARTED

PLANNING YOUR TRIP

Planning a trip to Romania involves careful consideration of various factors to ensure a seamless and enjoyable experience. Here's a step-by-step guide to help you plan your adventure:

1. Research and Itinerary: Research Romania's diverse regions, historical sites, and attractions. Create a rough itinerary based on your interests, whether it's exploring castles, hiking in the mountains, or immersing yourself in local culture.

2. Best Time to Visit: Consider the weather and your preferred activities. The summer months (June to August) offer pleasant weather, while winter (December to February) is ideal for winter sports enthusiasts. Spring and autumn are great for cultural and outdoor activities.

3. Travel Documents: Ensure your passport is valid for at least six months beyond your planned departure date. Check visa requirements for your nationality and obtain necessary permits if required.

4. Health Precautions: Consult your healthcare provider for recommended vaccinations and health precautions. Carry a basic first aid kit and any necessary medications.

5. Travel Insurance: Purchase travel insurance that covers medical emergencies, trip cancellations, and other unforeseen events. It provides peace of mind in case of unexpected situations.

6. Budget and Currency: Determine your budget and plan your expenditures accordingly. Familiarize yourself with the local currency (Romanian leu) and have a mix of cash and cards for payments.

7. Accommodation: Research and book accommodations in advance, especially during peak tourist seasons. Choose from a variety of options, including hotels, guesthouses, and hostels, based on your preferences and budget.

8. Transportation: Decide on your mode of transportation within Romania. Renting a car offers flexibility, but public transportation, including trains and buses, is extensive and efficient.

9. Language: Learn basic Romanian phrases to facilitate communication. While many Romanians speak English, locals appreciate visitors making an effort to speak their language.

10. Cultural Sensitivity: Familiarize yourself with Romanian customs and etiquette to respect local traditions. Be open-minded and embrace the cultural differences you encounter.

11. Activities and Experiences: Research and book tours, activities, and experiences in advance, especially for popular attractions. Consider local guided tours to gain insights into the country's history and culture.

12. Pack Wisely: Pack appropriate clothing for the season and your planned activities. Don't forget essentials like comfortable walking shoes, a travel adapter, and a portable charger.

By meticulously planning your trip, you'll be well-prepared to make the most of your time in Romania, ensuring a memorable and rewarding travel experience.

BEST TIME TO VISIT

The best time to visit Romania depends on your preferences and the type of experience you're seeking:

1. **Summer (June to August):** Summer is the peak tourist season in Romania. The weather is warm and pleasant, making it ideal for outdoor activities, festivals, and exploring the countryside. Popular tourist destinations are lively during this time, but be prepared for larger crowds and higher prices.

2. **Spring (April to May) and Autumn (September to October):** These shoulder seasons offer mild weather, blooming landscapes in spring, and vibrant foliage in autumn. It's an excellent time for outdoor activities like hiking and exploring historic sites. Prices are generally lower, and you'll

encounter fewer tourists, allowing for a more relaxed experience.

3. Winter (December to February): Winter is perfect for winter sports enthusiasts. Romania's ski resorts, especially in the Carpathian Mountains, offer excellent conditions for skiing and snowboarding. Christmas markets in cities like Bucharest and Sibiu are also popular attractions during this time. If you enjoy winter activities and festive atmospheres, this is the best time for your visit.

Consider your preferred activities and weather conditions when planning your trip. Whether you want to enjoy the lively atmosphere of summer festivals, the tranquility of spring blooms, the beauty of autumn foliage, or the thrill of winter sports, Romania offers unique experiences throughout the year.

VISA AND ENTRY REQUIREMENTS

Before traveling to Romania, it's essential to understand the visa and entry requirements based on your nationality. Here's a general overview:

1. European Union (EU) and Schengen Area Citizens: Citizens of EU member states and Schengen Area countries do not need a visa to enter Romania. They can stay for an unlimited period, but they need a valid passport or national ID card.

2. Non-EU Citizens: Non-EU citizens may require a visa to enter Romania. The requirements vary based on the country of origin. It's advisable to check the official website of the Romanian Ministry of Foreign Affairs or the nearest Romanian embassy or consulate for the most up-to-date information regarding visa requirements.

3. Visa-Free Regime: Romania has visa-free agreements with several countries, allowing their citizens to enter Romania for short stays (usually up to 90 days) without a visa. However, the exact duration of stay and conditions can vary, so it's essential to check the specific agreements applicable to your nationality.

4. Extension of Stay: If you wish to extend your stay in Romania, you must apply for a residence permit. It's crucial to start the application process before your initial visa-free period expires.

5. Required Documents: When applying for a visa or entering Romania, you may need to provide documents such as a valid passport, proof of accommodation, travel itinerary, travel insurance, and proof of financial means to support your stay. Check the specific requirements corresponding to your situation.

It's highly recommended to verify the most current visa and entry requirements well in advance of your planned travel dates. Adhering to the regulations ensures a smooth entry into Romania, allowing you to focus on enjoying your trip without any complications.

CURRENCY AND MONEY MATTERS

The official currency of Romania is the Romanian leu, abbreviated as RON. Here are some key points about currency and managing your finances during your visit to Romania:

1. Currency Exchange: You can exchange your foreign currency to Romanian leu at banks, exchange offices, and some hotels. It's advisable to compare exchange rates and fees to get the best value for your money. Major credit cards (such as Visa and MasterCard) are widely accepted in hotels, restaurants, and larger shops in urban areas.

2. ATMs: Automated Teller Machines (ATMs) are readily available in cities and towns. They dispense Romanian leu and, in some cases, euros. Using local ATMs can be a convenient way to withdraw cash at a favorable exchange rate. However, be cautious of hidden fees that your home bank might charge for international withdrawals.

3. Credit Cards: Credit and debit cards are commonly accepted in urban areas and tourist destinations. However, it's a good practice to carry some cash, especially in rural areas, smaller towns, and local markets, where cash payments are preferred.

4. Tipping: Tipping is appreciated but not mandatory in Romania. In restaurants, if a service charge is not included, leaving a tip of around 10% is customary. It's polite to round up taxi fares and leave small change for services like hotel staff and porters.

5. Budgeting: Romania is generally more affordable compared to Western European countries. Your budget should consider accommodation, meals, transportation, activities, and souvenirs. Researching average costs for your planned activities can help you plan your budget effectively.

6. Safety: While Romania is a safe country, it's advisable to keep your money, passport, and other valuables secure. Consider using a money belt or a neck pouch to carry your essentials, especially in crowded areas.

7. Currency Symbols: The Romanian leu is represented by the symbol "RON." For example, 1 leu is written as "1 RON."

By being mindful of currency exchange rates, using ATMs strategically, and being aware of tipping customs, you can manage your finances effectively during your stay in Romania.

CHAPTER 2: DISCOVERING ROMANIA

HISTORICAL LANDMARKS

Romania is a treasure trove of historical landmarks, each with its unique story and architectural marvels. Here are some must-visit historical landmarks in Romania:

1. Bran Castle: Commonly known as Dracula's Castle, this imposing fortress in Transylvania is a blend of history and legend. Explore its rooms and corridors to learn about its medieval heritage and the Dracula mythology.

2. Peles Castle: Nestled in the Carpathian Mountains, Peles Castle is a masterpiece of German Renaissance architecture. It served as a royal residence and is renowned for its intricate woodwork, stained glass windows, and opulent decor.

3. Corvin Castle: Also known as Hunyadi Castle, this Gothic-Renaissance castle in Hunedoara is one of Romania's most impressive fortresses. Its grand halls, towers, and drawbridges offer a glimpse into medieval life.

4. Sibiu Historic Center: Sibiu, a city in Transylvania, boasts a well-preserved medieval historic center. Wander through its cobblestone streets, explore the Council Tower, and visit the Brukenthal National Museum to experience the city's rich history.

5. Painted Monasteries of Northern Moldova: These UNESCO World Heritage Sites feature monasteries adorned with vibrant frescoes depicting religious scenes. Voronet Monastery, with its iconic blue hue, is one of the most famous among them.

6. Densus Church: Known as the oldest stone church in Romania, Densus Church dates back to the 7th century. Its ancient stone walls and unique architecture make it a fascinating historical site.

7. Merry Cemetery: Located in the village of Sapanta, this cemetery is unlike any other. Instead of somber gravestones, colorful wooden crosses depict scenes from the lives of the deceased, creating a cheerful and unique atmosphere.

8. The Dacian Fortresses of the Orastie Mountains: These ancient fortresses, built by the Dacians more than 2,000 years ago, are UNESCO World Heritage Sites. Explore the impressive ruins of Sarmizegetusa Regia and learn about the fascinating Dacian history.

9. The Palace of the Parliament: Situated in Bucharest, this colossal building is the world's heaviest and most expensive administrative building. It offers guided tours, allowing visitors to marvel at its extravagant architecture and learn about its complex history.

Exploring these historical landmarks will transport you back in time, offering a deep understanding of Romania's rich and diverse heritage.

VIBRANT CITIES

Romania is home to several vibrant cities, each with its unique character, cultural attractions, and lively atmosphere. Here are some of the most vibrant cities in Romania that you should consider exploring:

1. Bucharest: The capital and largest city of Romania, Bucharest is a bustling metropolis known for its eclectic architecture, historic sites, vibrant nightlife, and thriving arts scene. Explore the old town (Lipscani), visit the massive Palace of the Parliament, and enjoy the city's diverse restaurants, cafes, and clubs.

2. Cluj-Napoca: Often referred to as Cluj, this city in the heart of Transylvania is a hub of culture and creativity. It hosts numerous festivals, art events, and concerts throughout the year. Cluj-Napoca is also known for its historic architecture, beautiful parks, and vibrant student population.

3. Timișoara: Known as the "City of Flowers" and the birthplace of the 1989 Romanian Revolution, Timișoara is a city with a rich history and a lively atmosphere. Explore its charming squares, historic buildings, and cultural venues. The city hosts various festivals, including the Timișoara Revolution Festival and the Timișoara Jazz Festival.

4. Sibiu: This city in Transylvania is famous for its well-preserved medieval architecture and charming old town. Sibiu hosts cultural events, theater festivals, and concerts, making it a vibrant destination for art enthusiasts. The city was designated the European Capital of Culture in 2007.

5. Iași: Located in northeastern Romania, Iași is a city of great historical and cultural significance. It's home to the oldest university in Romania and boasts elegant architecture, museums, and theaters. Iași is also known for its lively nightlife, with numerous bars, clubs, and cafes.

6. Brașov: Nestled in the Carpathian Mountains, Brașov is a picturesque city with a vibrant atmosphere. Explore the medieval old town, visit the Black Church, and enjoy outdoor activities like hiking and skiing in the nearby mountains. The city hosts various events, including the Braşov International Film Festival & Market.

7. Constanţa: Romania's main port city on the Black Sea coast, Constanţa offers a unique blend of historical sites, modern architecture, and beach resorts. Explore the ancient ruins of Tomis, relax on the sandy beaches, and experience the city's lively nightlife during the summer months.

Each of these cities has its own charm and cultural offerings, making them vibrant destinations for travelers seeking a diverse range of experiences in Romania.

PICTURESQUE TOWNS AND VILLAGES

Romania is dotted with picturesque towns and villages that exude charm, history, and natural beauty. Exploring these idyllic places offers a glimpse into the country's rich cultural heritage. Here are some of the most picturesque towns and villages in Romania:

1. Sibiu: Known for its well-preserved medieval architecture, Sibiu boasts colorful houses, cobblestone streets, and charming squares. The town's Old Town area and the Bridge of Lies are must-see attractions.

2. Sighişoara: This medieval citadel town is famous for its well-preserved 16th-century buildings. Sighişoara is the birthplace of Vlad the Impaler (Dracula) and is recognized as a UNESCO World Heritage Site.

3. Biertan: Located in Transylvania, Biertan is renowned for its fortified church, a UNESCO World Heritage Site. The village is surrounded by vineyards and rolling hills, creating a picturesque backdrop.

4. Viscri: A small village famous for its fortified church and traditional Saxon houses. Viscri offers a peaceful atmosphere and a glimpse into rural Romanian life.

5. Maramureş Wooden Churches: The Maramureş region is known for its wooden churches, eight of which are UNESCO World Heritage Sites. These churches feature intricate woodwork and are nestled amidst stunning landscapes.

6. Bran: Aside from the famous Bran Castle, the surrounding area is dotted with charming villages. Bran village itself is picturesque, with traditional houses and the Carpathian Mountains in the background.

7. Moieciu de Jos: This village is surrounded by the Bucegi Mountains and is known for its stunning natural beauty. It's an excellent base for hiking and exploring the nearby Piatra Craiului National Park.

8. Râşnov: Nestled between the Bucegi and Piatra Craiului Mountains, Râşnov is a scenic town with a well-preserved medieval fortress offering panoramic views of the surroundings.

9. Bucovina Painted Monasteries: The villages surrounding the Painted Monasteries of Northern Moldova, such as Gura Humorului and Suceviţa, are picturesque and offer a unique blend of art and tradition.

10. Cheia: Tucked away in the Carpathian Mountains, Cheia is a tranquil village surrounded by forests and hiking trails. It's an ideal destination for nature lovers and those seeking a peaceful retreat.

Exploring these towns and villages allows you to experience the authentic charm of rural Romania, where history, culture, and natural beauty come together in perfect harmony.

NATURAL WONDERS

Romania is a country of diverse and breathtaking natural wonders, ranging from majestic mountains to pristine lakes and unique geological formations. Here are some of Romania's most remarkable natural wonders:

1. Carpathian Mountains: This mountain range stretches across Romania, offering excellent opportunities for hiking, skiing, and exploring scenic landscapes. The Făgăraş Mountains, part of the Southern Carpathians, are especially stunning and home to Romania's highest peak, Moldoveanu.

2. Danube Delta: Europe's largest and best-preserved delta, the Danube Delta is a UNESCO World Heritage Site. It's a paradise for birdwatchers and nature enthusiasts, with its maze of waterways, reed beds, and diverse wildlife, including pelicans and rare species of fish.

3. Bucegi Mountains: Located in the Southern Carpathians, the Bucegi Mountains are known for their dramatic rock formations, including the Sphinx and Babele, natural rock sculptures created by erosion. These formations are a popular hiking destination.

4. Retezat National Park: A designated UNESCO Biosphere Reserve, Retezat National Park is a haven for biodiversity. It's home to rare plants, animals, and glacial lakes, making it a paradise for nature lovers and hikers.

5. Turda Gorge: This limestone gorge, located in the Apuseni Mountains, offers stunning hiking trails, caves, and rock formations. The gorge is especially magical during autumn when the foliage turns vibrant shades of red and gold.

6. Scarisoara Ice Cave: One of the largest ice caves in the world, Scarisoara Ice Cave houses a massive ice block that remains frozen throughout the year. It's a unique natural phenomenon located in the Apuseni Mountains.

7. Bâlea Lake: Nestled in the Făgăraş Mountains, Bâlea Lake is a glacial lake surrounded by picturesque landscapes. It's accessible via a scenic cable car ride and is a popular starting point for hiking trails.

8. Sphinx and Babele: As mentioned earlier, these rock formations in the Bucegi Mountains are a natural wonder. The Sphinx resembles the famous Egyptian Sphinx, while Babele, meaning "The Old Women," are uniquely shaped rocks resembling old women.

9. Muddy Volcanoes: The Berca Mud Volcanoes are a rare geological phenomenon located in the Subcarpathian hills. These miniature volcanoes spew mud instead of lava, creating a lunar-like landscape.

10. Cheile Nerei-Beușnița National Park: This national park is known for its pristine rivers, waterfalls, and lush forests. The Beușnița Waterfall and the Bigăr Waterfall are highlights of the park, offering spectacular natural beauty.

Exploring these natural wonders allows you to witness the awe-inspiring beauty and diversity of Romania's landscapes, making it a paradise for outdoor enthusiasts and nature lovers.

CHAPTER 3: EXPERIENCING ROMANIAN CULTURE

ROMANIAN CUISINE

Romanian cuisine is a delightful fusion of flavors, influenced by various cultures and regions. Here are some key elements and dishes that define the richness of Romanian culinary traditions:

1. Hearty Stews: Romanian cuisine is known for its hearty stews, with "mici" (grilled sausages) and "mititei" being popular choices. Sarmale, cabbage rolls stuffed with minced meat and rice, cooked in a tomato-based sauce, are a cherished dish often served during special occasions.

2. Mămăligă: This traditional Romanian polenta is made from cornmeal and often served as a side dish, complementing stews, sausages, or cheese. It's a staple in Romanian cuisine and is similar to Italian polenta.

3. Soups: Romanian soups are flavorful and diverse. Ciorbă, a sour soup made with vegetables and meat, is a popular choice. It often includes ingredients like sorrel, borscht, or lemon juice to add a tangy flavor.

4. Mici: Mici, or mititei, are small sausages made from a mixture of minced meats (usually beef, lamb, and pork) and spices. They are grilled and often served with mustard, fresh bread, and pickles. Mici are a favorite during barbecues and social gatherings.

5. Mămăligă cu Brânză și Smântână: Mămăligă served with cheese and sour cream is a comforting dish. Mămăligă is a type of cornmeal porridge, and when combined with cheese and sour cream, it creates a delicious and filling meal.

6. Ciorbă de Perișoare: This soup features meatballs made from a mixture of minced meat, rice, and spices, cooked in a sour broth with vegetables. It's a flavorful and satisfying soup enjoyed across Romania.

7. Desserts: Romanian desserts include a variety of pastries, cakes, and sweet breads. One popular dessert is "cozonac," a sweet bread filled with nuts, cocoa, and spices, often enjoyed during holidays and celebrations.

8. Drob: Drob is a traditional Easter dish made from lamb organs, usually liver, heart, and lungs, mixed with greens and spices. It's baked in the oven and served as a festive appetizer.

9. Elderflower Cordial (Socată): Socată is a refreshing traditional Romanian drink made from elderflowers. It's a fermented beverage with a slightly sweet and tangy taste, enjoyed especially during the summer months.

Romanian cuisine is a delightful exploration of flavors, with an emphasis on hearty dishes and fresh, locally sourced ingredients. It reflects the country's rich culinary heritage and is sure to satisfy any food lover's palate.

TRADITIONAL DISHES AND DELICACIES

Romanian cuisine offers a diverse range of traditional dishes and delicacies, reflecting the country's history, culture, and regional influences. Here are some more traditional dishes and delicacies that you might find in Romania:

1. Sarmale: Sarmale are cabbage rolls stuffed with a mixture of minced meat (usually pork), rice, onions, and spices. They are often served with mămăligă (cornmeal porridge) and sour cream, creating a hearty and flavorful meal.

2. Mici (Mititei): Mici are small sausages made from a blend of minced meats (such as beef, pork, and lamb) seasoned with garlic, black pepper, and other spices. They are grilled and served with mustard, fresh bread, and pickles.

3. Mămăligă cu Brânză și Smântână: Mămăligă, a type of cornmeal porridge, is often served with brânză (cheese), smântână (sour cream), and sometimes a fried egg on top. It's a staple dish in Romanian cuisine and is both comforting and delicious.

4. Ardei Umpluți: Ardei umpluți are bell peppers stuffed with a mixture of minced meat, rice, onions, and spices. The stuffed peppers are simmered in a tomato-based sauce until tender and flavorful.

5. Mici: Mici, or mititei, are small sausages made from a mixture of minced meats (usually beef, lamb, and pork) and spices. They are grilled and often served with mustard, fresh bread, and pickles. Mici are a favorite during barbecues and social gatherings.

6. Drob de Miel: Drob de miel is a traditional Romanian Easter dish made from lamb organs, usually liver, heart, and lungs, mixed with greens, onions, and spices. It's seasoned and baked in the oven, creating a flavorful and festive dish.

7. Bulz: Bulz is a dish made from mămăligă mixed with brânză (cheese) and sometimes bacon. The mixture is shaped into balls and baked or grilled until golden and crispy. It's a simple yet tasty dish enjoyed in various regions of Romania.

8. Plăcinte: Plăcinte are savory pastries filled with ingredients like cheese, potatoes, cabbage, or pumpkin. They are often baked until golden and flaky, making them a popular snack or breakfast option.

9. Zacuscă: Zacuscă is a flavorful vegetable spread made from roasted eggplants, red peppers, onions, and tomatoes. It's seasoned with garlic and spices, creating a delicious condiment often enjoyed with bread or as a side dish.

10. Papanași: Papanași are traditional Romanian doughnuts, typically made from a mixture of cottage cheese, semolina, eggs, and flour. They are fried until golden, then topped with sour cream and jam, creating a sweet and indulgent dessert.

These traditional dishes and delicacies showcase the rich culinary heritage of Romania, offering a delightful culinary experience for anyone eager to explore the country's flavors.

LOCAL RESTAURANTS AND FOOD MARKETS

When exploring Romania, experiencing local cuisine at traditional restaurants and food markets is a delightful way to immerse yourself in the country's culinary culture. Here are some recommendations for local restaurants and food markets in various regions of Romania:

1. Bucharest:

- **Caru' cu Bere:** This historic restaurant in Bucharest offers a traditional Romanian ambiance and serves classic dishes like sarmale, mici, and various soups.

- **La Mama:** La Mama is a popular restaurant chain in Bucharest, known for its homely atmosphere and authentic Romanian cuisine, including hearty stews and grilled meats.

- **Obor Market:** One of Bucharest's largest and oldest markets, Obor Market offers a wide range of fresh produce, meats, cheeses, and local snacks. It's an excellent place to experience daily life and sample local delicacies.

2. Cluj-Napoca:

- **Roata:** Roata is a charming restaurant in Cluj-Napoca, offering traditional Transylvanian dishes with a modern twist. Their menu includes regional specialties and creative reinterpretations of classic recipes.

- **Piata Cibin:** This lively food market in Cluj-Napoca features stalls selling fresh fruits, vegetables, local cheeses, and pastries. It's a great spot to sample local produce and street food.

3. Timişoara:

- **Casa Bunicii (Grandma's House):** A cozy restaurant in Timişoara serving homemade Romanian dishes prepared with love and care. The menu includes traditional soups, stews, and desserts.

- **Piaţa Agroalimentară (Agricultural Market):** This bustling market offers a wide variety of fresh produce, meats, cheeses, and baked goods. It's a great place to explore local flavors and buy ingredients for a picnic.

4. Brasov:

- **Sergiana:** Sergiana is a well-known restaurant in Brasov, offering a menu filled with Romanian specialties. The restaurant is famous for its sarmale, grilled meats, and local desserts.

- **Piaţa Sfatului:** Brasov's main square hosts a food market where you can find local products, traditional snacks, and handmade crafts. It's a vibrant place to sample regional foods and enjoy the lively atmosphere.

5. Constanta (Black Sea Coast):

- **La Scoica Land:** Located near the Black Sea, this seafood restaurant in Constanta offers a variety of fresh fish, mussels, and other seafood dishes. The restaurant provides a picturesque seaside dining experience.

- **Tomis Market:** Tomis Market in Constanta is a lively market where you can find a variety of seafood, fruits, vegetables, and local snacks. It's a great place to taste the flavors of the Black Sea region.

Exploring these local restaurants and food markets will give you the opportunity to savor the authentic tastes of Romanian cuisine while immersing yourself in the country's vibrant food culture.

FESTIVALS AND EVENTS

Romania hosts a variety of festivals and events throughout the year, celebrating its rich cultural heritage, music, art, and traditions. Here are some notable festivals and events in Romania:

1. George Enescu Festival: Held in Bucharest, the George Enescu Festival is one of the world's most prestigious classical music events. It features renowned orchestras, conductors, and soloists, paying tribute to the famous Romanian composer George Enescu.

2. Sibiu International Theatre Festival: This festival takes place in Sibiu, showcasing theatrical performances from around the world. The historic city provides a unique backdrop for the diverse array of plays, performances, and street theater acts.

3. Transilvania International Film Festival (TIFF): TIFF is one of the largest film festivals in Eastern Europe, held annually in Cluj-Napoca. It features a wide selection of international and Romanian films, attracting filmmakers, actors, and cinephiles from across the globe.

4. Untold Festival: Untold is Europe's largest electronic music festival, taking place in Cluj-Napoca. It features top DJs and artists, attracting music enthusiasts from all over the world. The festival creates a vibrant atmosphere with its impressive stage designs and light shows.

5. Mărțișor: Celebrated on March 1st, Mărțișor marks the arrival of spring in Romania. People exchange small decorative tokens called "mărțișoare," symbolizing good luck and the coming of warmer days. This tradition is deeply rooted in Romanian culture.

6. Romanian Wine Festival: Held in various cities, the Romanian Wine Festival celebrates the country's rich winemaking heritage. Visitors can sample a wide range of Romanian wines, learn about different grape varieties, and enjoy traditional food pairings.

7. Horezu Pottery Fair: This fair, held in the town of Horezu, showcases the renowned Horezu ceramics, which is recognized as a UNESCO Intangible Cultural Heritage. Visitors can admire and purchase intricately crafted pottery, attend workshops, and learn about this traditional craft.

8. Rosia Montana Film Festival: This environmental and human rights film festival takes place in Rosia Montana, addressing social and environmental issues through film screenings, discussions, and cultural events.

9. Medieval Festival Sibiu: Sibiu hosts a vibrant Medieval Festival, where the historic city center transforms into a medieval marketplace. Visitors can enjoy reenactments, jousting tournaments, traditional crafts, and medieval-inspired performances.

10. Rasnov Fortress Film Evenings: Rasnov Fortress hosts outdoor film screenings during the summer months, allowing visitors to enjoy movies against the backdrop of the ancient fortress walls, creating a unique cinematic experience.

Attending these festivals and events provides an opportunity to immerse yourself in Romania's culture, art, and traditions, offering memorable experiences and a deeper understanding of the country's heritage.

ARTS AND CRAFTS

Romania boasts a rich tradition of arts and crafts, reflecting its diverse cultural heritage and skilled artisans. Here are some notable arts and crafts traditions in Romania:

1. Traditional Embroidery: Romanian embroidery is famous for its intricate patterns and vibrant colors. Different regions have distinct embroidery styles, and this craft is often seen on traditional clothing, home textiles, and accessories.

2. Wood Carving: Wood carving is a cherished craft in Romania, producing beautifully carved items such as furniture, religious artifacts, decorative objects, and even traditional masks used in local festivities.

3. Pottery: Romanian pottery is known for its rustic charm and intricate designs. Various regions have their unique pottery styles, with motifs often inspired by nature and folklore. Visitors can find decorative plates, bowls, and figurines.

4. Icon Painting: Icon painting is a traditional art form in Romania, with skilled artists creating religious icons adorned with intricate details and rich colors. These icons are often used in churches and homes for religious purposes.

5. Folk Art and Textiles: Romanian folk artists create a wide range of crafts, including woven textiles, rugs, baskets, and decorative items. These crafts often feature traditional patterns and techniques, passed down through generations.

6. Egg Painting (Pisanki or Ouă Încondeiate): Romanian artisans are skilled in the art of decorating eggs, a tradition especially prominent during Easter. Intricate designs are created using wax and dyes, resulting in beautifully patterned eggs.

7. Traditional Mask Making: Various regions in Romania have unique mask-making traditions, especially related to local festivals and celebrations. These masks are often colorful and elaborate, representing characters from folklore and mythology.

8. Glass Painting: Glass painting is a traditional craft in Romania, where skilled artists create delicate and colorful designs on glass items such as vases, plates, and decorative glassware.

9. Leatherwork: Romanian artisans are known for their leatherworking skills, creating items like belts, wallets, bags, and footwear. These products often feature intricate tooling and traditional designs.

10. Rug Weaving: Romanian rugs are renowned for their quality and diverse designs.

Each region has its unique weaving style and patterns, producing rugs that are not only functional but also works of art.

Exploring local markets, craft fairs, and artisan workshops in Romania provides an opportunity to admire and purchase these exquisite handmade crafts, allowing visitors to take a piece of Romania's artistic heritage home with them.

CHAPTER 4: OUTDOOR ADVENTURES

HIKING AND TREKKING ROUTES

Romania is a paradise for hikers and nature enthusiasts, offering a diverse range of hiking and trekking routes that cater to various skill levels. Here are some spectacular hiking and trekking destinations in Romania:

1. Retezat Mountains: Retezat National Park is a hiker's dream, featuring a network of trails that lead to glacial lakes, waterfalls, and alpine meadows. The route to Bucura Lake, the largest glacial lake in Romania, is particularly scenic.

2. Făgăraş Mountains: Known as the "Transylvanian Alps," the Făgăraş Mountains offer challenging trails, including the Făgăraş Ridge Trail, which traverses the highest peaks in Romania. The route provides breathtaking views and an exhilarating trekking experience.

3. Piatra Craiului Mountains: Piatra Craiului National Park offers stunning limestone formations and diverse flora and fauna. The Piatra Craiului Ridge Trail is a popular route, offering panoramic views of the surrounding landscapes.

4. Bucegi Mountains: The Bucegi Mountains are known for their dramatic rock formations, including the Sphinx and Babele. Hiking trails like the Bucegi Circuit provide opportunities to explore these natural wonders and enjoy the scenic beauty of the region.

5. Apuseni Mountains: The Apuseni Mountains are a treasure trove of caves, waterfalls, and picturesque landscapes. The Padis Plateau offers various hiking trails, and the Scarisoara Ice Cave is a unique attraction worth exploring.

6. Ceahlău Massif: Ceahlău National Park is home to the "Holy Mountain of Romania," known for its cultural and natural significance. The Dochia Cabin to Toaca Peak trail offers a challenging yet rewarding hike, with panoramic views from the summit.

7. Bicaz Gorge: Bicaz Gorge is a spectacular canyon in the Eastern Carpathians, offering hiking trails that lead through narrow passageways and alongside the Bicaz River. The Red Lake (Lacul Roşu) area nearby provides additional hiking opportunities.

8. Rodna Mountains: Rodna National Park is known for its diverse landscapes, including alpine meadows, glacial lakes, and rugged peaks. The trek to Pietrosu Peak, the highest peak in the Eastern Carpathians, offers panoramic views and a challenging ascent.

9. Cozia National Park: Cozia National Park is characterized by dense forests, limestone cliffs, and the Olt River. The Cozia Massif offers various trails, including routes to Cozia Monastery and the picturesque Turnu Monastery.

10. Maramureş Mountains: Maramureş Mountains are located in the northern part of Romania and offer serene trails, traditional villages, and a peaceful atmosphere. The Gutâi Mountains, part of the Maramureş range, provide excellent hiking routes.

Before embarking on any hiking or trekking adventure, it's essential to be well-prepared, follow safety guidelines, and check weather conditions. Local guides and park authorities can provide valuable information about the best routes and current trail conditions.

SKIING AND WINTER SPORTS

Romania offers excellent opportunities for skiing and winter sports enthusiasts, with several ski resorts nestled in the Carpathian Mountains. Here are some popular skiing destinations in Romania:

1. Poiana Braşov: Poiana Braşov is one of Romania's most famous ski resorts, located near the city of Braşov. It offers well-groomed slopes suitable for skiers of all levels, from beginners to advanced. The resort provides skiing and snowboarding lessons, equipment rental, and a vibrant après-ski scene.

2. Sinaia: Sinaia is a charming resort town located at the base of the Bucegi Mountains. The resort is known for its scenic slopes and the Peleş Castle, a beautiful royal residence. The slopes cater to both beginners and experienced skiers, offering a variety of trails.

3. Predeal: Predeal is the highest town in Romania and a popular destination for winter sports. It has several ski slopes, and the surrounding Bucegi and Piatra Mare Mountains provide a picturesque backdrop for skiing and snowboarding activities.

4. Busteni: Busteni is another ski resort located near Sinaia, offering a range of slopes with varying levels of difficulty. Visitors can enjoy not only skiing and snowboarding but also breathtaking views of the Carpathian Mountains.

5. Straja: Straja is a ski resort located in the Parâng Mountains, known for its challenging slopes and vibrant nightlife. It attracts both professional skiers and snowboarders looking for thrilling experiences on the slopes.

6. Arieseni: Arieseni is a ski resort in the Apuseni Mountains, popular for its family-friendly atmosphere and affordable skiing options. The resort is suitable for beginners and intermediate skiers, making it an ideal choice for families and casual skiers.

7. Rânca: Rânca is a ski resort situated in the Parâng Mountains, offering a mix of easy and challenging slopes. The resort's location provides stunning views of the surrounding peaks, creating a picturesque setting for winter sports enthusiasts.

8. Vatra Dornei: Vatra Dornei, located in the Northern Carpathians, is a well-known ski resort in Northern Romania. It features a range of slopes and winter activities, making it a popular destination for skiers and snowboarders seeking diverse terrain.

Before hitting the slopes, make sure to check the weather conditions, ski resort facilities, and safety guidelines. Many resorts offer equipment rental and skiing lessons, making it accessible for beginners and those looking to improve their skills.

CYCLING TRAILS

Romania offers a diverse range of cycling trails, from scenic routes through picturesque countryside to challenging mountain trails for experienced cyclists. Here are some notable cycling trails and destinations in Romania:

1. Transfagarasan Highway: Known as one of the most spectacular roads in the world, the Transfagarasan Highway offers a challenging cycling route through the Făgăraş Mountains. The road winds through breathtaking landscapes, including waterfalls, glacial lakes, and alpine meadows.

2. Transalpina Road: Often referred to as the "King's Road," Transalpina is the highest mountain road in Romania. It offers a thrilling cycling experience with winding roads, hairpin turns, and panoramic views of the Parâng Mountains.

3. Maramureş County: Maramureş, located in the northern part of Romania, provides scenic cycling routes through charming villages, wooden churches, and rolling hills. The region's rural beauty and traditional architecture make it a delightful destination for cyclists.

4. Apuseni Mountains: The Apuseni Mountains offer cycling trails that pass through forests, caves, and traditional villages. Cyclists can explore the natural wonders of the region, including the Scarisoara Ice Cave and the Turda Gorges, while enjoying the tranquil countryside.

5. Danube Cycle Path: The Danube Cycle Path follows the Danube River, offering a relatively flat and scenic route through Romania. Cyclists can enjoy the river views, visit historic towns like Orşova and Drobeta-Turnu Severin, and explore the diverse landscapes along the way.

6. Braşov and Surroundings: Braşov and its surroundings provide various cycling trails suitable for different skill levels. Cyclists can explore the medieval charm of Braşov, ride through the nearby Piatra Mare Mountains, or venture into the Bucegi Mountains for more challenging routes.

7. Râşnov Fortress to Bran Castle: This cycling route takes you from Râşnov Fortress to Bran Castle, passing through scenic landscapes and historic sites. The route offers a mix of paved roads and off-road trails, allowing cyclists to experience the beauty of the Carpathian Mountains.

8. Ciuc Mountains: The Ciuc Mountains in Harghita County offer cycling trails with diverse terrain, including forested slopes and alpine meadows. The trails provide opportunities for both leisurely rides and more adventurous mountain biking experiences.

Before embarking on a cycling adventure, it's essential to check trail conditions, weather forecasts, and safety guidelines. Romania's cycling trails provide an excellent opportunity to explore the country's natural beauty and cultural heritage on two wheels.

WATER SPORTS AND ACTIVITIES

Romania, with its diverse waterways, lakes, and coastline along the Black Sea, offers a variety of water sports and activities for enthusiasts. Here are some popular water sports and activities you can enjoy in Romania:

1. Kayaking and Canoeing: Romania's rivers, including the Danube, offer great opportunities for kayaking and canoeing. Explore the serene waters, navigate through gentle rapids, and enjoy the scenic beauty along the riverbanks.

2. Rafting: For adrenaline seekers, several rivers in Romania, such as Buzău and Bistriţa, offer thrilling rafting experiences. Professional guides and outfitters organize rafting trips suitable for various skill levels.

3. Windsurfing and Kitesurfing: The Black Sea coast, especially around Mamaia Beach, is popular for windsurfing and kitesurfing. With consistent winds and sandy beaches, it's an ideal location for both beginners and experienced surfers.

4. Sailing: Romania's Black Sea coastline provides opportunities for sailing enthusiasts. Explore the open sea, enjoy the sea breeze, and take in the beautiful coastal scenery aboard a sailboat.

5. Jet Skiing: Jet skiing is a popular activity along the Black Sea Coast. Rental services are available, allowing visitors to experience the thrill of speeding over the waves and enjoying the freedom of the open sea.

6. Scuba Diving: Discover the underwater world of the Black Sea by scuba diving. Various dive sites along the coast offer the chance to explore marine life, underwater rock formations, and even sunken wrecks.

7. Fishing: Romania's rivers and lakes are abundant with fish, making it an excellent destination for fishing enthusiasts. Obtain the necessary permits and enjoy fishing for species like trout, carp, and pike in scenic natural settings.

8. Cruises and Boat Tours: Take a leisurely cruise on the Danube River and explore the scenic landscapes, charming villages, and historical sites along the way. Boat tours are available on the Danube Delta as well, allowing you to experience the unique biodiversity of the delta.

9. Wakeboarding: Wakeboarding is a popular water sport on Romania's lakes and rivers. Enthusiasts can enjoy the excitement of gliding over the water while being towed by a boat, cable, or winch.

10. Canyoning: Experience the thrill of canyoning in Romania's gorges, where you can navigate through water-filled canyons, rappel down waterfalls, and swim in natural pools. It's a challenging and adventurous activity for nature lovers.

Before engaging in any water sports activities, ensure your safety by wearing appropriate gear, following instructions from experienced guides, and being aware of local regulations and weather conditions. Romania's water sports scene offers something for everyone, from relaxing cruises to adrenaline-pumping adventures.

CHAPTER 5: PRACTICAL INFORMATION

TRANSPORTATION

Romania offers various modes of transportation, making it accessible for both travelers within the country and those exploring different regions. Here's an overview of transportation options in Romania:

1. Public Transportation:

   - **Buses and Trams:** Most cities and towns have a well-developed network of buses and trams, making it convenient for commuting within urban areas.

   - **Metro:** Bucharest has an efficient metro system, offering a quick way to travel within the city and avoid traffic congestion.

- **Trolleybuses:** Trolleybuses are common in many cities, providing an eco-friendly mode of transportation.

2. Taxis: Taxis are readily available in urban areas. Make sure to use licensed taxis or reputable ride-sharing services for a safe and reliable journey. Always check the fare on the meter or agree on a price before starting the ride.

3. Trains: Romania has an extensive rail network connecting major cities and towns. Trains are a comfortable and scenic way to travel, especially for longer distances. There are different classes of trains, including InterCity (IC) trains, which offer faster and more comfortable journeys.

4. Renting a Car: Renting a car is a convenient option, especially if you plan to explore rural areas or visit multiple destinations. Romania's road network is generally good, allowing for a flexible travel experience. However, be prepared for varying road conditions in some regions.

5. Bicycles: Many cities in Romania, including Bucharest and Cluj-Napoca, have dedicated bike lanes and bike-sharing programs. Cycling is a great way to explore urban areas and enjoy the scenic countryside.

6. Domestic Flights: While Romania is well-connected by roads and railways, there are domestic flights available for traveling longer distances quickly. However, domestic flights are not as common as other modes of transportation.

7. Rental Scooters and Electric Bikes: In some cities, you can find rental services for electric scooters and bikes, providing a convenient and eco-friendly way to explore urban areas.

8. Danube River Cruises: For a unique travel experience, consider taking a river cruise on the Danube River. Several cruise companies offer trips along the Danube, allowing you to explore picturesque landscapes and visit riverside towns and attractions.

9. Public Ferries: Romania's Danube Delta region has public ferries and boats that transport passengers between various villages and natural attractions within the delta.

When using public transportation, it's helpful to check schedules and routes in advance. For intercity travel, especially during peak seasons, it's advisable to book train tickets or other transportation services in advance to secure your journey.

ACCOMMODATION OPTIONS

Romania offers a wide range of accommodation options to suit various preferences and budgets. Whether you're looking for luxury hotels, charming boutique guesthouses, budget-friendly hostels, or unique countryside cottages, Romania has something for every traveler. Here are some popular accommodation options you can consider:

1. Hotels: Romania has a diverse selection of hotels ranging from luxurious five-star establishments in major cities like Bucharest and Cluj-Napoca to comfortable mid-range hotels and budget-friendly options in various tourist destinations. Hotels often provide amenities such as restaurants, spas, and recreational facilities.

2. Pensions and Guesthouses: Traditional Romanian pensions, known as "pensiuni," and guesthouses offer a cozy and intimate atmosphere. These accommodations are often family-run and provide personalized services. They are prevalent in rural areas, offering a chance to experience local hospitality.

3. Boutique Hotels: Boutique hotels in Romania are known for their unique charm, stylish interiors, and personalized services. They are often located in historic buildings and offer a more intimate and upscale experience for travelers seeking a touch of luxury.

4. Hostels: Hostels are popular among budget travelers and backpackers. Romania's major cities and tourist destinations have hostels that provide affordable dormitory-style accommodations, communal spaces, and a social atmosphere. Hostels are a great option for meeting fellow travelers.

5. Holiday Rentals and Apartments: Vacation rentals and apartments are available in many cities and tourist areas. Platforms like Airbnb offer a variety of options, including private apartments, cottages, and villas. Renting a holiday home can be an excellent choice for families or groups looking for more space and privacy.

6. Countryside Cottages: Romania's countryside offers unique accommodation experiences, including traditional cottages and farmstays. Staying in a countryside cottage allows you to immerse yourself in the rural way of life, enjoy homemade meals, and explore the natural surroundings.

7. Rural Guesthouses: Rural guesthouses, often located in picturesque villages and near natural attractions, provide a tranquil retreat away from urban hustle. They offer a chance to experience local traditions, enjoy organic food, and participate in outdoor activities.

8. Resorts: Romania's coastal area along the Black Sea is home to resorts offering beachfront accommodations, spa facilities, and various recreational activities. These resorts are popular during the summer months, providing a relaxing beach holiday experience.

9. Monastery Accommodations: Some monasteries in Romania offer accommodation for visitors, providing a unique opportunity for travelers interested in religious and cultural experiences. Staying in a monastery allows you to learn about Orthodox traditions and enjoy a peaceful environment.

Before booking accommodation, consider your preferences, budget, and the location's proximity to attractions and activities. It's advisable to read reviews and check the facilities offered by the accommodation to ensure a comfortable stay during your visit to Romania.

SAFETY AND HEALTH TIPS

When traveling to Romania, it's essential to prioritize your safety and health. Here are some safety and health tips to keep in mind during your visit:

1. Travel Insurance: Before traveling, consider purchasing travel insurance that covers medical expenses, trip cancellations, and emergencies. This ensures you have financial protection in case of unforeseen events.

2. Emergency Numbers: Know the local emergency numbers, including 112, which is the general emergency number in Romania. This number can be dialed for police, fire, medical emergencies, and search and rescue services.

3. Healthcare: Romania has a relatively good healthcare system, especially in major cities. However, it's advisable to have travel insurance that covers medical emergencies. Carry any necessary prescription medications and a basic first aid kit.

4. Water: While tap water is generally considered safe to drink in most urban areas, it's recommended to drink bottled or filtered water, especially in rural regions. Avoid ice in your drinks if you're uncertain about the water source.

5. Food Safety: Romanian cuisine is delicious, but make sure to eat at reputable restaurants and avoid street food if you have a sensitive stomach. Ensure that meat and seafood are thoroughly cooked. Be cautious about dairy products in rural areas.

6. Insect Protection: In forested or rural areas, protect yourself from ticks and mosquitoes. Wear long sleeves, long pants, and use insect repellent. Check for ticks after spending time outdoors, as they can transmit diseases like Lyme disease.

7. Sun Protection: If you're traveling during the summer, wear sunscreen, sunglasses, and a hat to protect yourself from the strong sun. Dehydration and heatstroke are risks, so drink plenty of water and stay in shaded areas during peak sun hours.

8. Currency and Valuables: Be mindful of your belongings, especially in crowded tourist areas. Use hotel safes to store valuables and carry only necessary items with you. Be cautious when using ATMs and avoid displaying large amounts of cash in public.

9. Traffic Safety: Be vigilant when crossing streets, as traffic can be hectic, especially in cities. Use designated crosswalks and pedestrian crossings. When driving, obey traffic rules and be aware of local driving habits.

10. Local Customs and Etiquette: Familiarize yourself with local customs and etiquette to show respect for the culture. Learn a few basic phrases in Romanian to communicate with locals, as it's appreciated.

11. COVID-19 Precautions: Stay updated on the latest travel advisories and COVID-19 guidelines issued by local authorities and international health organizations. Follow recommended safety measures, including wearing masks indoors and in crowded areas, practicing social distancing, and frequent handwashing.

By staying informed, taking necessary precautions, and being aware of your surroundings, you can ensure a safe and enjoyable experience while traveling in Romania.

CHAPTER 6: BEYOND TOURISM

VOLUNTEERING OPPORTUNITIES

Volunteering in Romania can be a rewarding way to contribute to local communities and immerse yourself in the country's culture. There are various volunteering opportunities available, ranging from social projects to environmental conservation initiatives. Here are some ways you can get involved in volunteering in Romania:

1. **Community Development:** Many organizations in Romania focus on community development projects, such as supporting underprivileged families, organizing educational programs for children, and assisting with healthcare initiatives.

Volunteering with these organizations allows you to directly impact the lives of local residents.

2. Environmental Conservation: Romania is known for its beautiful natural landscapes. There are conservation projects dedicated to preserving the country's biodiversity, protecting wildlife, and promoting sustainable practices. Volunteers often participate in activities like reforestation, wildlife monitoring, and environmental education.

3. Animal Welfare: Several animal shelters and organizations in Romania work towards the welfare of stray animals. Volunteers can help with animal care, rehabilitation, and adoption initiatives. Working with these organizations can be fulfilling for animal lovers.

4. Teaching and Education: Volunteer programs in Romania offer opportunities to assist in schools, community centers, or orphanages. Volunteers can teach English, provide tutoring, or organize extracurricular activities to enhance the educational experiences of local children and youth.

5. Cultural Exchange: Volunteering programs that focus on cultural exchange allow volunteers to engage with local communities, learn about traditional Romanian customs, and share their own culture. These programs often involve organizing cultural events, workshops, and language exchange activities.

6. Archaeological Excavations: Romania has a rich history, and archaeological projects welcome volunteers to participate in excavations, artifact preservation, and historical research. This is a unique opportunity for history enthusiasts and aspiring archaeologists.

7. NGOs and Non-Profit Organizations: Many non-governmental organizations (NGOs) in Romania work on various social and environmental issues. Volunteering with these organizations can involve activities such as advocacy, fundraising, event planning, and community outreach.

8. Farming and Sustainable Living: Volunteers interested in sustainable agriculture and organic farming can find opportunities to work on farms, participate in permaculture projects, and promote eco-friendly practices in rural communities.

When considering volunteering opportunities, it's essential to research the organizations thoroughly, understand the scope of the projects, and inquire about accommodation, meals, and support provided to volunteers. Additionally, ensure that you have the necessary visas or permits if you're volunteering for an extended period. Volunteering can be a meaningful way to make a positive impact while experiencing the warmth and hospitality of the Romanian people.

RESPONSIBLE TOURISM INITIATIVES

Responsible tourism initiatives in Romania focus on promoting sustainable practices, preserving the environment, supporting local communities, and respecting cultural heritage. Here are some responsible tourism initiatives and practices in Romania:

1. **Ecotourism:** Romania's diverse natural landscapes, including the Carpathian Mountains and the Danube Delta, make it an excellent destination for ecotourism. There are initiatives promoting responsible hiking, wildlife conservation, and eco-friendly accommodations to minimize the environmental impact of tourism.

2. Rural Tourism: Rural tourism initiatives encourage visitors to stay in traditional guesthouses, farmsteads, and cottages in rural areas. These accommodations are often family-run, providing income to local communities. Travelers can experience authentic Romanian culture and contribute directly to the local economy.

3. Wildlife Conservation: Organizations and national parks in Romania work on wildlife conservation projects, protecting endangered species and preserving natural habitats. Responsible tourists can support these initiatives through guided tours, donations, and volunteering opportunities.

4. Waste Management: Responsible tourism initiatives promote proper waste disposal and recycling practices. Some accommodations and tour operators have adopted eco-friendly measures, such as reducing plastic usage, recycling, and encouraging guests to participate in clean-up activities.

5. Cultural Heritage Preservation: Responsible tourism includes respecting cultural heritage sites, historical monuments, and traditional customs. Travelers are encouraged to be mindful of local traditions, dress codes, and etiquettes when visiting cultural and religious sites.

6. Community Engagement: Engaging with local communities is a key aspect of responsible tourism. Travelers can participate in community-based projects, support local artisans, and purchase handmade crafts, contributing to the livelihoods of local residents.

7. Educational Initiatives: Responsible tourism organizations and tour operators often organize educational programs, workshops, and guided tours to raise awareness about environmental conservation, wildlife protection, and cultural heritage preservation. Tourists can participate in these activities to learn about local ecosystems and traditions.

8. Sustainable Food Practices: Supporting restaurants and accommodations that prioritize local and organic ingredients promotes sustainable agriculture. Farm-to-table experiences allow travelers to enjoy fresh, locally sourced meals and support farmers and producers in the region.

9. Low-Impact Activities: Responsible tourists can engage in low-impact activities such as birdwatching, nature photography, and hiking with certified guides. These activities promote appreciation for natural beauty without disturbing wildlife or damaging ecosystems.

10. Volunteering: Many responsible tourism organizations offer volunteering opportunities, allowing travelers to actively participate in conservation, community development, and educational projects. Volunteering fosters a deeper connection with the destination and contributes meaningfully to local initiatives.

By choosing responsible tourism options and being mindful of your environmental and cultural impact, you can contribute to the sustainable development of tourism in Romania while enjoying a meaningful and authentic travel experience.

LEARNING ROMANIAN LANGUAGE AND CULTURE

Learning the Romanian language and culture can greatly enhance your travel experience in Romania. Here are some tips to help you get started:

1. Language Learning Apps: Use language learning apps like Duolingo, Babbel, or Rosetta Stone to practice Romanian vocabulary and basic phrases. These apps offer interactive lessons and exercises to improve your language skills.

2. Online Language Courses: Enroll in online language courses or find language tutors who can provide personalized lessons through platforms like iTalki or Preply. Having a tutor can help you practice speaking and listening skills.

3. Language Exchange: Participate in language exchange programs where you can teach English or your native language to a

Romanian speaker in exchange for learning Romanian. Websites like Tandem and ConversationExchange can help you find language partners.

4. Local Language Classes: If you're staying in Romania for an extended period, consider taking language classes at a local language school or cultural center. Many cities offer classes for beginners and advanced learners.

5. Immerse Yourself: Surround yourself with the language as much as possible. Watch Romanian movies, listen to Romanian music, and follow Romanian social media accounts. Immersion helps improve your understanding of the language's rhythm and pronunciation.

6. Practice with Locals: Don't be afraid to practice speaking with locals. Most Romanians appreciate your effort to learn their language and will be supportive. Engaging in conversations with native speakers will enhance your conversational skills.

7. Learn Cultural Etiquette: Understanding Romanian cultural norms and etiquette is as important as learning the language. Familiarize yourself with social customs, greetings, and dining etiquette to show respect for the local culture.

8. Attend Cultural Events: Attend cultural events, festivals, and local gatherings to experience Romanian traditions firsthand. Participating in cultural events provides insights into the country's customs, music, dance, and cuisine.

9. Read Romanian Literature: Reading books, newspapers, or online articles in Romanian can help you expand your vocabulary and comprehension skills. Start with simple texts and gradually progress to more complex materials.

10. Travel and Explore: Traveling within Romania allows you to practice your language skills in various regions with different dialects and accents. Engaging with locals in different cities and villages will expose you to diverse linguistic nuances.

11. Be Patient and Persistent: Learning a new language takes time and effort. Be patient with yourself, practice regularly, and don't be afraid to make mistakes. Persistence and consistency are key to language learning success.

By combining language learning with cultural immersion, you'll gain a deeper understanding of Romanian culture and language, making your travel experience more enriching and enjoyable.

CHAPTER 7: APPENDIX

USEFUL PHRASES IN ROMANIAN

Certainly! Here are some useful phrases in Romanian that can help you communicate effectively during your travels:

Basic Phrases:
1. **Hello:** Bună (BOO-nuh)
2. **Goodbye:** La revedere (lah reh-veh-DEH-reh)
3. **Please:** Te rog (teh ROHG)
4. **Thank you:** Mulţumesc (mool-tsoo-MESK)
5. **You're welcome:** Cu plăcere (koo PLAH-cheh-reh)
6. **Yes:** Da (dah)
7. **No:** Nu (noo)
8. **Excuse me / I'm sorry:** Scuzaţi-mă (SKOO-zah-tzuh-muh)

9. What is your name?: Cum vă numiți? (koom vuh NOO-mits?)

10. My name is...: Numele meu este... (NOO-meh-leh MEOO eh-STE...)

11. Where is the bathroom?: Unde este baia? (OON-deh YEH-steh BAH-yah?)

12. How much does it cost?: Cât costă? (caht KOHS-tuh?)

13. I need help: Am nevoie de ajutor (ahm neh-VOY-eh deh ah-ZHOO-tohr)

14. I don't understand: Nu înțeleg (noo uhn-TSEH-lehg)

15. Good morning: Bună dimineața (BOO-nuh dee-mee-neh-TSAH-tzuh)

16. Good afternoon: Bună ziua (BOO-nuh ZEE-wah)

17. Good evening: Bună seara (BOO-nuh SEH-ah-rah)

18. Good night: Noapte bună (NWAHP-teh BOO-nuh)

Travel and Directions:

19. Where is the train station?: Unde este gara? (OON-deh YEH-steh GAH-rah?)

20. Where can I find a taxi?: Unde pot găsi un taxi? (OON-deh pot GUH-see oon TAHK-see?)

21. I'm lost: M-am rătăcit (mahm ruh-tuh-CHEET)

22. Can you help me?: Puteți să mă ajutați? (poo-TEHTS sah muh ah-ZHOO-tsuhts?)

23. How can I get to...?: Cum pot ajunge la...? (koom pot ah-JOON-geh lah...?)

24. Left: Stânga (STUHNG-uh)

25. Right: Dreapta (DREH-ahp-tuh)

26. Straight ahead: Drept înainte (DREHPT uhn-INAIH-teh)

Dining and Food:

27. Menu: Meniu (meh-NEE-oo)

28. Water: Apă (AH-puh)

29. Coffee: Cafea (cah-FEH-ah)

30. I'm a vegetarian: Sunt vegetarian (soont veh-geh-tah-REE-ahn)

31. The bill, please: Nota de plată, vă rog (NOH-tah deh PLAH-tuh, vuh ROHG)

Emergency Phrases:

32. Help: Ajutor (ah-ZHOO-tohr)

33. Police: Poliție (poh-LEET-syeh)

34. Doctor: Doctor (DOHK-tohr)

35. Hospital: Spital (SPEE-tahl)

36. I need a pharmacy: Am nevoie de o farmacie (ahm neh-VOY-eh deh oh fahr-mah-CYEH)

Remember to practice these phrases and don't hesitate to use them when needed. Most Romanians appreciate visitors trying to speak their language. Enjoy your time in Romania!

EMERGENCY CONTACTS

In case of emergencies in Romania, dial the universal emergency number:

Emergency Services: 112

This number can be dialed for police, fire, medical emergencies, and search and rescue services. When calling 112, be prepared to provide clear information about the nature of the emergency and your location to ensure a swift response from the authorities.

Additionally, here are some specific emergency contact numbers in Romania:

Police: 955

Fire Department: 961

Ambulance: 961 or 112

These numbers can be dialed directly for the respective emergency services. It's essential to know these contacts and keep them readily accessible during your stay in Romania.

SAMPLE ITINERARIES

Here are two sample itineraries for exploring Romania, catering to different interests: one for history and culture enthusiasts and another for nature lovers and outdoor enthusiasts.

Sample Itinerary 1: History and Culture Exploration

Day 1-2: Bucharest
- Explore the historic Old Town of Bucharest, including landmarks like the Palace of the Parliament and Stavropoleos Monastery.
- Visit the Village Museum (Muzeul Satului) to experience traditional Romanian architecture and culture.

- Enjoy Romanian cuisine at local restaurants and try traditional dishes like sarmale (stuffed cabbage rolls) and mici (grilled sausages).

Day 3-4: Sibiu
- Explore Sibiu's well-preserved medieval old town, known for its charming squares and historic buildings.
- Visit the Brukenthal National Museum and the ASTRA Museum of Traditional Folk Civilization.
- Walk along the Liar's Bridge and enjoy panoramic views of the city.

Day 5-6: Brasov and Bran
- Explore Bran Castle, often associated with the Dracula legend.
- Visit the Black Church (Biserica Neagră) and the Council Square in Brasov.

- Hike or take a cable car to the top of Tampa Mountain for stunning views of the city.

Day 7-8: Sighisoara and Cluj-Napoca
- Explore the medieval citadel of Sighisoara, a UNESCO World Heritage Site.
- Visit the Clock Tower and the birthplace of Vlad the Impaler.
- Travel to Cluj-Napoca, a vibrant city known for its historical sites and lively cultural scene.
- Visit the Botanical Garden and the Matthias Corvinus House.

Day 9-10: Maramures
- Explore the picturesque region of Maramures, known for its wooden churches and traditional villages.
- Visit the Merry Cemetery (Cimitirul Vesel) in Sapanta, famous for its colorful tombstones.

- Experience the local way of life and try regional dishes like mămăligă (cornmeal porridge) and cârnați (sausages).

Sample Itinerary 2: Nature and Outdoor Adventure

Day 1-3: Bucharest and Danube Delta
- Spend a day exploring Bucharest's cultural attractions.
- Travel to the Danube Delta, a UNESCO Biosphere Reserve and a paradise for birdwatching and nature lovers.
- Take a boat tour to explore the delta's unique ecosystem, rich in wildlife and diverse bird species.

Day 4-5: Brasov and Piatra Mare Mountains

- Explore Brasov and visit nearby natural attractions like the Seven Ladders Canyon and the Rasnov Fortress.
- Hike in the Piatra Mare Mountains, known for their scenic trails and waterfalls.
- Experience outdoor activities like rock climbing and zip-lining.

Day 6-7: Bucegi Mountains and Sibiu

- Trek in the Bucegi Mountains, a beautiful area with challenging trails and breathtaking views.
- Visit Sibiu and explore its surrounding natural wonders like the Cindrel Mountains and the Dumbrava Sibiului Natural Park.
- Enjoy outdoor adventures such as cycling and horseback riding.

Day 8-9: Retezat National Park

- Travel to Retezat National Park, home to diverse flora and fauna, alpine lakes, and hiking trails.

- Explore the park, hike to Bucura Lake, and witness the stunning landscapes of the Carpathian Mountains.

- Participate in guided nature walks and wildlife spotting activities.

Day 10: Return to Bucharest

- Return to Bucharest and spend your last day relaxing or exploring any remaining attractions in the city.

Feel free to adjust these itineraries based on your interests, travel pace, and the time you have available. Romania offers a wealth of experiences for both history enthusiasts and nature lovers, ensuring a memorable and diverse travel adventure.

PACKING CHECKLIST

Creating a packing checklist is crucial to ensure you have everything you need for a comfortable and enjoyable trip to Romania. Here's a comprehensive packing checklist to help you prepare for your journey:

Essentials:
- **Passport, Visa, and Travel Documents:** Ensure they are valid for the duration of your stay.
- **Travel Insurance:** Carry a copy of your travel insurance policy and emergency contact numbers.
- **Money:** Cash, credit/debit cards, and a money belt or secure pouch for valuables.

- **Travel Adapter:** A universal adapter to charge your electronic devices.

- **Prescription Medications:** Along with a copy of your prescriptions.

- **Health Insurance Card:** If applicable.

- **Language Guidebook or Mobile App:** For quick translations and communication assistance.

- **Travel Itinerary:** Printed or saved digitally on your phone.

Clothing:

- **Comfortable Walking Shoes:** Suitable for exploring cities and natural sites.

- **Lightweight and Breathable Clothing:** Especially during the summer months.

- **Weather-Appropriate Clothing:** Layers for cooler evenings and rainproof gear.

- **Swimwear:** If you plan to visit pools or beaches.

- Hat and Sunglasses: For sun protection.

- Socks and Underwear: Enough for the duration of your trip.

- Pajamas or Sleepwear: Depending on your accommodation preferences.

Toiletries:
- Toothbrush and Toothpaste
- Shampoo and Conditioner
- Soap or Body Wash
- Deodorant
- Hairbrush/Comb
- Razor/Shaving Kit
- Sunscreen
- Lip Balm with SPF

- Personal Medications and First Aid Kit:
Bandages, pain relievers, antiseptic wipes, etc.

Electronics:

- Mobile Phone and Charger
- Camera and Charger
- Power Bank for recharging your devices on the go.
- Earphones/Headphones
- Portable Wi-Fi device If necessary for internet access.

Miscellaneous:

- **Daypack or Small Backpack:** For day trips and carrying essentials.
- **Reusable Water Bottle:** Stay hydrated and reduce plastic waste.
- **Snacks:** Especially if you have dietary preferences or restrictions.
- **Travel Towel:** Quick-drying and compact for convenience.
- **Travel Umbrella:** Lightweight and portable, in case of rain.

- **Travel Locks:** For securing your luggage.

- **Notebook and Pen:** For jotting down notes or journaling.

- **Ziploc Bags:** Useful for storing snacks, wet clothes, or toiletries.

- **Local Guidebooks or Maps:** Physical or digital versions for navigating.

Optional Items:

- **Travel Pillow and Eye Mask:** For comfortable rest during flights or long journeys.

- Insect Repellent

- **Travel Laundry Detergent:** If planning to do laundry during your trip.

- Travel Sewing Kit

- Hand Sanitizer

Remember to tailor this checklist based on the specific activities and destinations you plan to visit in Romania. Be mindful of the weather conditions and any special events you might attend during your stay. Safe travels!

CHAPTER 8: RESOURCES

USEFUL WEBSITE AND APPS

There are several useful websites and apps that can enhance your travel experience in Romania. Here's a list of some recommended ones:

Websites:

1. Romania Tourism

(https://www.romaniatourism.com/): The official website for Romania's tourism board, offering comprehensive information about destinations, attractions, and travel tips.

2. TripAdvisor

(https://www.tripadvisor.com/): A popular platform for traveler reviews and recommendations for hotels, restaurants, and attractions in Romania.

3. Booking.com

(https://www.booking.com/): A leading platform for booking accommodations worldwide, including hotels, guesthouses, and vacation rentals in Romania.

4. Rome2rio

(https://www.rome2rio.com/): A travel planning website that helps you find the best way to get from one place to another, including various transportation options in Romania.

5. Couchsurfing

(https://www.couchsurfing.com/): Connect with locals and fellow travelers for cultural exchange, events, and sometimes free accommodation.

6. Weather Underground

(https://www.wunderground.com/): Check the weather forecast for specific cities in Romania to plan your activities accordingly.

Apps:

1. Google Maps (iOS/Android): Offers detailed maps, real-time traffic updates, and directions, making it useful for navigation in Romania.

2. Duolingo (iOS/Android): A language learning app that offers Romanian lessons to help you pick up basic phrases and vocabulary.

3. XE Currency (iOS/Android): Provides live currency exchange rates, useful for converting your home currency to Romanian Lei (RON).

4. TripAdvisor (iOS/Android): The mobile app version of the website, allowing you to read reviews, find restaurants, and plan activities on the go.

5. Booking.com (iOS/Android): Book accommodations, view reservation details, and find last-minute deals using the app.

6. Uber (iOS/Android) / Bolt (iOS/Android): Ride-sharing apps available in some Romanian cities for convenient and affordable transportation.

7. Trainline (iOS/Android): Book train tickets and check schedules for traveling within Romania and to neighboring countries.

8. WhatsApp (iOS/Android): A popular messaging app that allows you to stay in touch with friends and family, especially if you have access to Wi-Fi.

9. Yelp (iOS/Android): Find local restaurants, cafes, and attractions with user reviews and ratings.

Remember to download these apps and check their functionality before your trip, especially if you plan to use them offline. Having these tools at your fingertips can significantly enhance your travel experience in Romania. Safe travels!

MAP OF ROMANIA

International boundary
County (județ) boundary
★ National capital
● County (județ) center
Railroad
Expressway
Other road
◈ Principal port

*București is a municipality
with county status.*

MAP OF ROMANIA
MAP CREDIT @ORANGESMILE

121

MAP OF SOME ROMANIAN CITIES

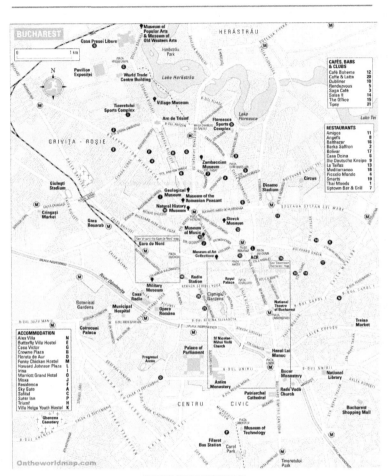

BUCHAREST CITY MAP
MAP CREDIT @bucharestmap360

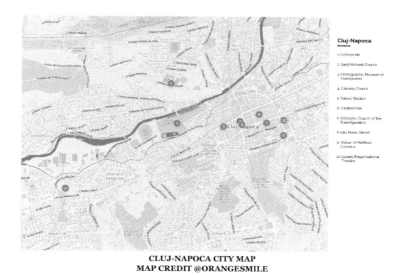

Cluj-Napoca
Romania

1 Fortress Hill

2 Saint Michael Church

3 Ethnographic Museum of Transylvania

4 Calvaria Church

5 Tailors' Bastion

6 Central Park

7 Orthodox Church of the Transfiguration

8 Iuliu Maniu Street

9 Statue of Matthias Corvinus

10 Lucian Blaga National Theatre

CLUJ-NAPOCA CITY MAP
MAP CREDIT @ORANGESMILE

TIMIȘOARA CITY MAP
MAP CREDIT @ORANGESMILE

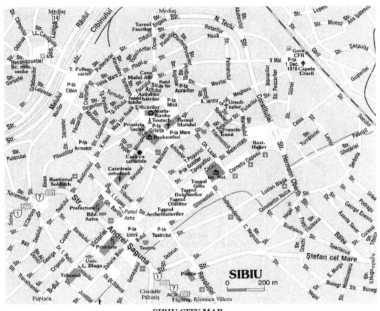

SIBIU CITY MAP
MAP CREDIT @TURKEY-VISIT

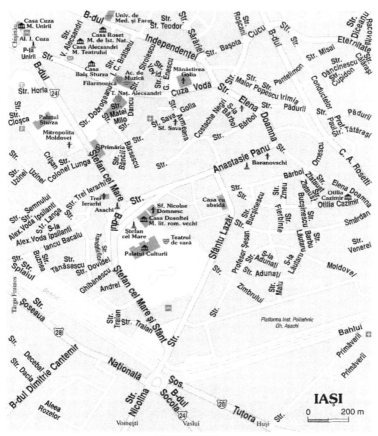

IASI CITY MAP
MAP CREDIT @WORLDMAP1

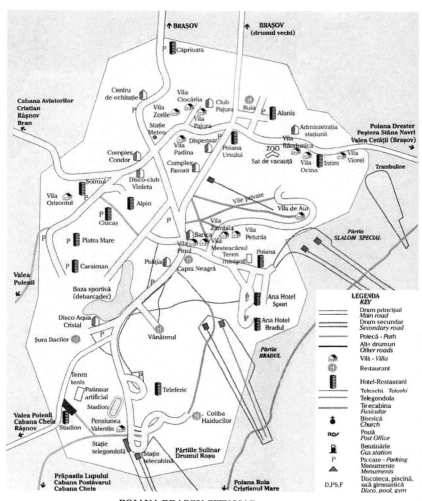

POIANA BRASOV CITY MAP
MAP CREDIT @SEJURURI

CONSTANȚA CITY MAP

MAP CREDIT @SYGICTRAVEL

CONCLUSION

As you prepare for your journey to Romania, you are embarking on an adventure filled with history, culture, natural beauty, and warm hospitality. Whether you're exploring ancient castles, hiking in the Carpathian Mountains, savoring traditional Romanian cuisine, or immersing yourself in vibrant cities, Romania has a wealth of experiences to offer.

Remember to embrace the local customs, try the delicious cuisine, and engage with the friendly people you'll meet along the way. Stay curious, be open to new experiences, and cherish the moments of discovery and connection. Your travels in Romania will undoubtedly leave you with lasting memories and a deeper understanding of this captivating country.

Wishing you a fantastic and enriching journey in Romania! If you have any more questions or need assistance in the future, don't hesitate to reach out. Safe travels and enjoy your adventure!

Printed in Great Britain
by Amazon

39042303R00078